The only lasting beauty is the beauty of the heart.

— RUMI

In Loving Memory

Compiled by DAN ZADRA

Art Direction by SARAH FORSTER

Designed by LIANNE ONART

To live in hearts
we leave behind
is not to die.

— THOMAS CAMPBELL

A GIFT for the
GRIEVING HEART

When someone we care about loses a loved one, we want to find a way to ease their sorrow—but how? Some things we just can't do for each other. We can't restore the loved one to life, or turn back the clock, or eliminate the pain. Often, we can't even find the right words to express the feelings overflowing in our hearts.

But there's one thing we can do. We can bring the one gift that requires no words, and which always triumphs over death. Quietly, faithfully, fervently, we can bring our love.

This, then, is our gift to the grieving heart. The messages in these pages remind us that grief's shadow eventually touches all of us. But the essential message is one of hope: life goes on, it must go on. In fact, it is by living out our lives, with the memories of our loved ones sheltered in our hearts, that we honor and cherish them most.

IN LOVING MEMORY

All who have been touched by beauty
are touched by sorrow at its passing.

— LOUISE CORDANA

IN LOVING MEMORY

I did not come to comfort you;
Only God can do that;
　　　but I did come to say
　　　how deeply and tenderly
　　　I feel for you...

— TRYON EDWARDS

In the deserts of the heart,
Let the healing fountain start.

— W. H. AUDEN

Go ahead and cry. I'll catch your tears.

— JILEEN RUSSELL

It has been said that there are several ways
to mourn. One is to weep; and we have done
our share of weeping.

Another way to mourn is to sing:
to sing a hymn to life, a life that still abounds
in sights and sounds and vivid colors...

We sing the songs of our beloved; we aspire
to their qualities of spirit; we take up their tasks
as they would have shouldered them.

— RABBI JACK STERN, JR.

Come on now, it helps to sing.

— SINGER JUDY COLLINS,
TO THE FRIENDS AND RELATIVES OF THE 230 LOVED ONES
WHO WENT DOWN ON TWA FLIGHT 800

Give sorrow words.

— WILLIAM SHAKESPEARE

The church is full. Many faces are unknown to me;
others are mileposts of my years.

I take a deep breath and pray one last time
for strength and composure to deliver his eulogy.

At the end, I borrow the words of a friend
who has walked this path before: "Daddy," she wrote,
"just follow the heading Peter Pan gave Wendy Darling.

As they surveyed the stars spread across the night sky,
he showed her the way like you have shown me:
'Second star to the right, then straight on 'till morning.'

Have a wonderful flight. We'll all meet you there."

— TAD BARTIMUS, FOR HER FATHER, JAMES

We are gathered together in her memory.

If you seek her memorial, look about you—
it's in the hearts of her family,
in the faces of her children,
in her writings and in her home.

— GEORGE A. CRILE,
REMEMBERING HIS WIFE, JANE

Not how did she die,
but how did she live?

Not what did she gain,
but what did she give?

Not, what was her church,
nor what was her creed,

But had she befriended
those really in need?

Not what did the words
in the newspaper say,

But how many were sorry
when she passed away?

— UNKNOWN

Because he lived,
there is more love in the world
than there would have been
without him.

And for him, that was the reason
above all others for the gift of life.

— NEW YORK TIMES,
A TRIBUTE TO MARTIN BUBER

Perhaps one of his beautiful children spoke
most simply and eloquently for us all.

Learning of his father's death, he said in
a tone of measureless loss, "He was so nice."
So he was. So he truly was.

— JOSEPH GALLAGHER,
FOR HIS BROTHER FRANCIS XAVIER GALLAGHER

Where is the good in goodbye?

— MEREDITH WILSON, "THE MUSIC MAN"

Don't be dismayed at goodbyes.
A farewell is necessary before
you can meet again.
And meeting again,
after moments or lifetimes,
is certain for those who are friends.

— RICHARD BACH

Everything science has taught me,
and continues to teach me,
strengthens my belief in the continuity
of our spiritual existence after death.

— WERNHER VON BRAUN

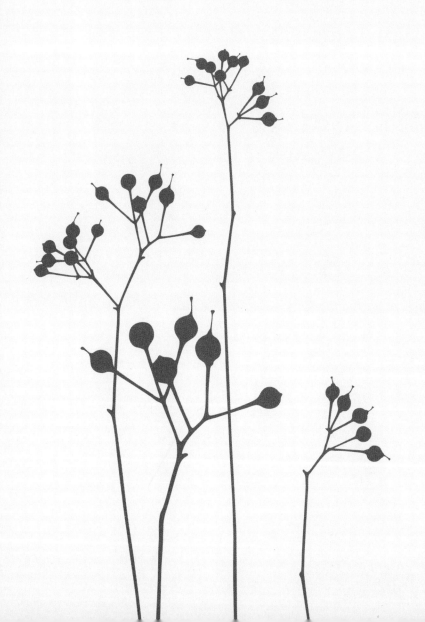

IN LOVING MEMORY

I don't care what they say...
Everybody knows that something is eternal.

And it ain't houses and it ain't names,
and it ain't earth, and it ain't even the stars...

Everybody knows in their bones
that something is eternal,
and that something has to do with
human beings.

All the greatest people ever lived have
been telling us that for five thousand years
and yet you'd be surprised how people
are always losing hold of it.

There's something way down deep
that's eternal about every human being.

— THORNTON WILDER, "OUR TOWN"

Death ends a life,
but not a relationship.

— JACK LEMMON

How long does a man live, after all...
And what do we mean when we say, 'gone forever'?

A man lives for as long as we carry him inside us,
for as long as we carry the harvest of his dreams,
for as long as we ourselves live,
holding memories in common, a man lives.

— BRIAN PATTEN

We talk about Heaven being so far away.
It is within speaking distance...

— DWIGHT L. MOODY

If I should ever leave you whom I love
To go along the Silent Way, grieve not,
Nor speak of me with tears, but laugh and talk
Of me as if I were beside you there…

And when you hear a song or see a bird
I loved, please do not let the thought of me
Be sad…For I am loving you just as
I always have…You were so good to me!

There are so many things I wanted still
To do—so many things to say to you…
Remember that I did not fear—it was
Just leaving you that was so hard to face…

We cannot see beyond…But this I know:
I loved you so—'twas heaven here with you!

— ISLA PASCHAL RICHARDSON

I'll keep finding things that are important,
and I'll know you put them there.

In life, you made my life complete;
in death you've left me life's intent.

Your love was wondrously given...
not to be saved, but spent.

— JANET VAUGHN

I find an old photograph
and see your smile.

As I feel your presence anew,
I am filled with warmth
and my heart remembers love.

I read an old card sent many years ago
during a time of turmoil and confusion.

The soothing words written then
still caress my spirit and bring me peace...

I remember you,

you are with me,

and I am not afraid.

— KIRSTI A. DYER

Sometimes the strong die too.

— LOUIS GOSSETT, JR.

When I was with my father,
when I was just a child,
the world was filled with wonder
and every place was wild.

And every day was magic,
and Santa Claus was true,
and all the things that mattered
were things my father knew.

We often went exploring...
and I learned to love the land,
but the greatest thing I ever learned
was how to understand—

That the finest gifts are often
things we may not always see;
when I wasn't with my father,
my father was with me.

— MARCIA JEFFREY HENDRICKSON

There are some
who bring a light so great to the world

that even after they have gone,
the light remains.

— UNKNOWN

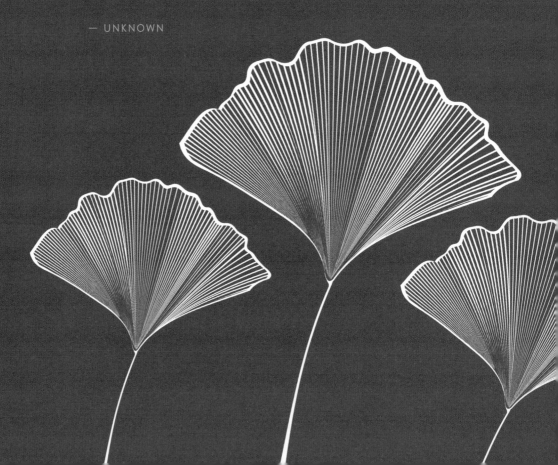

I've seen the promised land.
And I may not get there with you

but I want you to know tonight
that we, as a people,
will get to the promised land...

— MARTIN LUTHER KING, ONE DAY BEFORE HE DIED

This disease caused all the greatness
in her to rise to the surface.

What I loved about her is that when
somebody is so much on the edge of life,
you only say the truth to them, and they
only say the truth to you.

I'd like to live as she did—diving at every day
and grabbing pleasure when you can.

— ACTRESS MARY STEENBURGEN,
REMEMBERING HER FRIEND, AIDS ACTIVIST ELIZABETH GLASER

Compassion is your pain
I feel in my heart.

— HOSPICE SAYING

I loved my friend.
He went away from me.
There's nothing more to say.

The poem ends
soft as it began—
I loved my friend.

— LANGSTON HUGHES

Death is no more than passing
from one room into another.

But there's a difference for me, you know.
Because in that other room
I shall be able to see.

— HELEN KELLER

One day, as I was ending a visit to his hospital room,
I sat down on the bed and leaned over his big old body
and hugged him for a while, saying into the bedcovers
that I wished there was something I could do for him.

He had an answer: "Just love me," he said.

I do.

— CHARLES TRUEHART, ON HIS FATHER, WILLIAM

The rugged old Norsemen spoke of death
as..."home-going"...

Myriads of rejoicing living creatures,
daily, hourly, perhaps every moment
sink into death's arms...

Trees towering in the sky,
braving storms of centuries,
flowers turning faces to the light
for a single day or hour,
having enjoyed their share
of life's feast—all alike pass on
and away under the law
of death and love.

Yet all are our brothers
and they enjoy life as we do,
share Heaven's blessings with us,
die and are buried in hallowed ground,
come with us out of eternity
and return into eternity.

— JOHN MUIR

The snow melts on the mountain
And the water runs down to the spring,
And the spring in a turbulent fountain,
With a song of youth to sing,
Runs down to the riotous river,
And the river flows to the sea,
And the water again
Goes back in rain
To the hills where it used to be...

And so at last,
When our life has passed
And the river has run its course,
It again goes back,
O'er the selfsame track,
To the mountain which was its source...
So we shall run the course begun
Till we reach the silent shore.
Then revisit earth in a pure rebirth
From the heart of the virgin snow.

— WILLIAM RANDOLPH HEARST

Do not stand at my grave and weep,
I am not there, I do not sleep.

I am a thousand winds that blow.
I am the diamond glints on snow.
I am the sunlight on ripened grain.
I am the gentle autumn rain.

When you wake in the morning hush,
I am the swift, uplifting rush
Of quiet birds in circling flight.
I am the soft starlight at night.

Do not stand at my grave and weep,
I am not there, I do not sleep.
Do not stand at my grave and cry,
I am not there, I did not die!

— MARY FRYE

They lived and laughed
and loved and left.

— JAMES JOYCE

"Then what has been the reason for all of this?"
Freddie continued to question.

"Why were we here at all if we only have to fall and die?"

Daniel answered in his matter-of-fact way,
"It's been about the sun and the moon.
It's been about happy times together.

It's been about the shade and the old people and the children.
It's been about colors in Fall.
It's been about seasons. Isn't that enough?"

That afternoon, in the golden light of dusk, Daniel let go.

He fell effortlessly.
He seemed to smile peacefully as he fell.

"Goodbye for now Freddie," he said.

— LEO BUSCAGLIA,
THE FALL OF FREDDIE THE LEAF

In love longing
I listen to the monk's bell.

I will never forget you
even for an interval

short as those between
the bell notes.

— IZUMI SHIKIBU

Why did this happen to me? we ask.

It happened partly because we were
fortunate enough to have loved someone.

Without love there would be no grief.

— JUNE CERZA KOLF

When you are sorrowful
look again in your heart,
and you shall see that in truth
you are weeping for that
which has been your delight.

— KAHLIL GIBRAN

The reason it hurts so much to separate
is because our souls are connected.

— NICHOLAS SPARKS

How do I love thee? Let me count the ways.

I love thee to the depth and breadth and height
My soul can reach, when feeling out of sight
For the ends of Being and ideal Grace...

I love thee with the breath,
Smiles, tears, of all my life!—and, if God choose,
I shall but love thee better after death.

— ELIZABETH BARRETT BROWNING

You will not see me,
so you must have faith.

I wait for the time when
we can soar together again,
both aware of each other.

Until then, live your life to
its fullest and when you need me,
just whisper my name in your heart,
I will be there.

— EMILY DICKINSON

In the night of death,
hope sees a star
and listening love
can hear the rustle of a wing.

— ROBERT GREEN INGERSOLL

In one of the stars,
    I shall be living,

In one of them,
    I shall be laughing,

and so it will be as if all the stars were laughing
when you look at the sky at night.

— ANTOINE DE SAINT-EXUPÉRY, "THE LITTLE PRINCE"

I leave you love.

— MARY MCLEOD BETHUNE

"But how do I live without you?" she cried.

I left all the world to you when I died:
Beauty of earth and air and sea;
Leap of a swallow or a tree;

Kiss of rain and wind's embrace;
Passion of storm and winter's face;

Touch of feather, flower, and stone;
Chiseled line of branch or bone:

Flight of stars, night's caravan;
Song of crickets—and of man—

All these I put in my testament,
All these I bequeathed you when I went.

"But how can I see them without your eyes
Or touch them without your hand?
How can I hear them without your ear,
Without your heart, understand?"

These too, these too
I leave to you!

— ANNE MORROW LINDBERG

In the midst of winter,
   I found there was, within me,
      an invincible summer.

— ALBERT CAMUS

I talked with mothers who had lost a child...

Every single one said death gave their lives
new meaning and purpose.

And who do you think prepared them
for the rough, lonely road
they had to travel?

Their dying child.

They pointed their mothers toward
the future and told them to keep going.

The children had already accepted
what their mothers were fighting to reject.

— ERMA BOMBECK

If there is ever a tomorrow
when we are not together...

there is something
you must remember:

You are braver than you believe,
stronger than you seem,
and smarter than you think.

But the most important thing is,
even if we're apart...

I'll always be with you.

— WINNIE THE POOH,
BY A.A. MILNE

Is this the end? I know it cannot be,
Our ships shall sail upon another sea;

New islands yet shall break upon our sight,
New continents of love

and truth

and might.

— JOHN WHITE CHADWICK

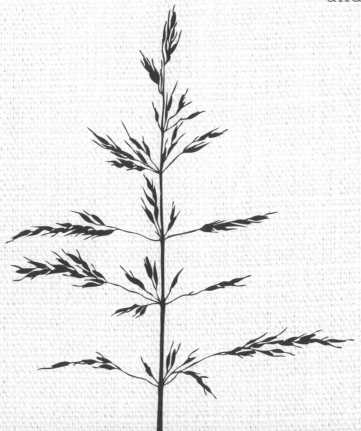

This is not the end, we'll meet again
God's promise will be kept,
But all the same, I feel no shame
in all the tears I've wept.

With God's own grace, I'll see your face
when it is my turn to die.
I loved you so, just that, no more;
for now, I'll say goodbye.

— FOREST R. WHATLEY

At the rising of the sun
and at its going down,
We remember them.

At the blowing of the wind
and in the chill of Winter,
We remember them.

At the opening of buds
and in the rebirth of Spring,
We remember them.

In the blueness of the sky
and in the warmth of Summer,
We remember them.

At the rustling of leaves
and in the beauty of Autumn,
We remember them.

In the beginning of the year
and when it ends,
We will remember them.

So long as we live,
they too shall live;
for they are now a part of us,
as we remember them.

— SYLVAN KAMENS & JACK RIEMER

COMPENDIUM®

live inspired

ACKNOWLEDGEMENTS

These quotations were gathered lovingly but unscientifically over several years and/or contributed by many friends or acquaintances. Some arrived—and survived in our files—on scraps of paper and may therefore be imperfectly worded or attributed. To the authors, contributors, and original sources, our thanks, and where appropriate, our apologies.

WITH SPECIAL THANKS TO THE ENTIRE COMPENDIUM FAMILY.

CREDITS:

Compiled by: Dan Zadra ✦ Designed by: Lianne Onart ✦ Art Direction by: Sarah Forster

ISBN: 978-1-935414-13-1

DEDICATED TO HOSPICE